HOW DO WE
KNOW
GOD EXISTS?

JOHN ANKERBERG

DILLON BURROUGHS

Advancing the Ministries of the Gospel

AMG *Publishers*

God's Word to you is our highest calling.

CONTENDERS BIBLE STUDY SERIES™

Contenders Bible Study Series
How Do We Know God Exists?

Published by AMG Publishers. All Rights Reserved.

First Printing, May 2008
ISBN 13: 978-089957-781-4

Editing by Rick Steele and Christy Graeber

Layout by PerfecType, Nashville, Tennessee

Cover Design by Indoor Graphics Corp., Chattanooga, Tennessee

Printed in Canada
13 12 11 10 09 08 –T– 6 5 4 3 2 1

Table of Contents

Session 6:

Foreword

By Dr. Norman Geisler

When Jude wrote his New Testament letter to Christians in the early church he felt compelled to urge his readers to "contend for the faith" (Jude 3). His words continue to provide a strong motivation for us today to understand the reasons behind what we believe both for our own personal growth and in order to communicate our faith to others.

The Contenders series of Bible study books by John Ankerberg and Dillon Burroughs is designed to provide a response for this tremendous need. As followers of Christ, we are instructed to be prepared to share the reason for our hope (1 Peter 3:15). In addition, those still seeking the truth regarding Jesus and the Word of God are encouraged, as the hearers of Paul in Berea were, to examine the Scriptures to discover if what they had been taught was true (Acts 17:11).

The innovative material found in this series can assist you in two specific ways. First, if you are already a believer in Christ, this series can provide answers to many of the complex questions you may be facing—or that you are asking yourself. Second, if you are a skeptic or seeker of spiritual truth contemplating what it means to follow Jesus Christ, this series can also help provide a factual basis for the Christian faith and the questions in your quest. You can feel free to wrestle with the difficult issues of the Christian faith in the context of friendly conversation with others. This is a powerful tool for individuals who sincerely desire to learn more about God and the amazing truths given to us in the Bible.

If you are one of the people who have chosen to participate in this new series, I applaud your efforts to grow in spiritual truth. Let the pages of this resource provide the basis for your journey as you learn more about contending for the faith we communicate in Jesus Christ.

Dr. Norman Geisler,
co-founder of Southern Evangelical Seminary
and author of seventy books, including the award-winning
Baker Encyclopedia of Christian Apologetics

Introduction

Welcome to the Contenders series! This small-group curriculum was developed with the conviction that claims about today's spiritual issues can and should be investigated. Christianity, sometimes stereotyped as non-intellectual and uneducated, is not allowed to make assertions of faith without providing practical answers why it should be taken seriously. If the Bible claims to be God's Word and claims to provide explanations for the most significant issues of life, both now and eternally, these assertions should be carefully examined. If this investigation proves these beliefs flawed, the only reasonable choice is to refuse to follow the Christian Scriptures as truth. However, if our investigation of the evidence leads to the discovery of truth, then the search will have been worthwhile. In fact, it will be life-changing.

Christians understand that God welcomes sincere seekers of truth. In fact, Jesus Christ Himself openly cheered such inquiry. The Bible is not a book shrouded in mystery, open to only a select group of experts. It is widely available for discussion and learning by anyone. The core beliefs of Christianity are publicly presented to anyone willing to consider their truths, whether skeptic, seeker, or life-long believer.

Consider this book your invitation. Investigate the choices, analyze the beliefs, and make your decisions. But be prepared—the truth you encounter is not another file to simply add to your collection. The truth of God's Word will transform every area of your life.

We often learn that we have mistakenly believed something that turns out to be false. We may even find ourselves not wanting to accept truth because it infringes upon our lifestyle or conflicts with long-held personal values. Through this series of discussion questions we will journey together to answer the question Pilate asked Jesus long ago: "What is truth?" (John 18:38). As authors, it is our hope that you will ultimately come to realize that Christian faith is based upon solid evidence worthy to build one's life upon. Whether you are currently still building your opinions on spiritual issues or are already a follower of Christ developing answers for your own questions and the questions of others, these guides will assist you on a captivating exploration of spiritual issues necessary in order to "contend for the faith" (Jude 3).

The Contenders Series for Your Group

The Contenders series is purposely designed to give truth seekers (those still investigating a relationship with Christ) an opportunity to ask questions and probe into the basics of Christianity within the friendly, caring environment of small-group discussion—typically in a group no larger than about a dozen people, with one or two individuals who serve as the discussion leaders. These leaders are responsible to coordinate the regular gatherings, build relationships with group members, and prepare to ask and answer questions, involving each person in the discussion. Through a combination of caring friendships, intelligent conversations, and genuine spiritual interest, it is our hope that these discussions will provide the basis for a fresh approach to exploring key concepts of Christian belief.

Because one of the intentions of this series is to address the real questions of the spiritual seeker, the questions are presented to represent the viewpoints of both the Christian and the skeptic. While the truths of Christianity are explicitly affirmed, hopefully many who join these discussions will find their own viewpoints understood and represented along the way. As seekers and skeptics feel valued in their current beliefs, they will be more open to honest discussion that leads to truth. The ultimate hope behind the Contenders series is that many who are seeking will come to know the truth about Christ, and that those who already follow Jesus will understand how to address the issues of their friends who are still exploring Christianity.

Of course, it is also important that those who already follow Jesus learn to grow in the basic beliefs of the Christian faith. As they do so, it will become easier to communicate the good news of the Christian faith in normal, everyday conversations with co-workers, neighbors, classmates, relatives, and even complete strangers. The process of struggling through these important issues and difficult questions will not only enhance one's own personal growth but also provide many specific details that can be used in everyday scenarios when the topic of faith arises with others.

Many groups will consist of some blend of believers and seekers. For example, your church may use this material for one of its small groups that consists mostly of people who already follow Christ. However, in the process, group members should feel comfortable and even encouraged to invite friends who have yet to begin a relationship with Christ. Special events designed to invite friends from outside of your current group, including simple social opportunities like dinner parties, a game night, movie night, or other activity should be considered. Regardless of the specific options selected, we pray that you will benefit tremendously as you use these

guides to connect through interactive discussions about the
issues of ultimate importance.

How to Use This Guide

Getting Started

At the start of each session is a segment of introductory
material, typically several paragraphs in length. Each par-
ticipant will want to read this information before the session
begins, even if it is read again when the group is together.
This "Getting Started" section is written with the skeptic in
mind, often including very controversial perspectives to stimulate challenging discussion. As a result, each person should
instantly feel the ability to share his or her viewpoint within
the safe context of a caring group of friends.

Talk about It

Next, each session includes a range of ten to twenty questions your group can use during discussion. Most groups will
find it impossible to use every single question every time. The
options are either to choose which questions best fit the needs
of your group, or to use the questions for more than one time
together. The key component of this "Talk about It" section
is to include each and every person, allowing the conversation
to help people process their thoughts on the issue.

Often, the opening question of each session is a simple opinion question. Through the use of this ice-breaker
approach, the conversation quickly takes off as each person
offers his or her thoughts on a non-threatening issue that
touches on the topic of the particular session. Certainly, the
creativity of the group may also provide additional or alterna-
tive ice-breaker questions or activities to start each session.
The goal is to achieve quick and enjoyable involvement by
everyone in the group.

Here's What I'm Thinking

The next section, called "Here's What I'm Thinking," transitions the time of discussion toward a more emotional element. The questions in this section deal directly with personal responses to the material in each session rather than just intellectual facts or opinions. This is a time to communicate what each person is feeling about the topic, since this is a critical step in helping a person come to a personal decision about the issue.

What Now?

In the "What Now?" section, participants are challenged to move beyond both intellectual and emotional responses toward personal application of the material shared in the session. Once each person has considered his or her personal position on the issue, the next part of the process is to determine how this position influences daily living. One interesting impact of this section is that each person will begin to understand the implications of both true and faulty beliefs, along with charting personal changes in belief formation from one session to the next.

Consider This

Each session also includes one or more segments called "Consider This," designed to provide additional factual material appropriate to each discussion. Each "Consider This" section is immediately followed by a question based on the material, so it's important (especially for leaders) to read and understand this part before each meeting.

What Others Have Said

Throughout each session, participants will discover various quotes on the topic of discussion. Rather than quoting primarily academic sources, these quotes provide diverse perspectives from those critical of the Christian faith and well-known personalities from today's culture, along with well-worded thoughts from some of today's top writers.

Additional Resources

At the end of each guide, we have provided a list of several resources from the authors on the issue. This is only an introduction to a vast array of print, audio, video, and electronic materials based on decades of research in these areas.

A Word to Discussion Leaders

One distinctive feature of the Contenders series is that the learning does not end with the material found in this book. The series website www.contendersseries.com is loaded with interactive links to numerous online articles, outside internet links, video clips, audio responses, and creative ways to help direct the discussions in your group. We hope you'll also find it to be an excellent personal study source as well. And if you still don't find the answer you're looking for, or just want to connect with the authors of this resource, you'll find a place where you can email your questions and other feedback for personal responses.

Creating Boundaries

These guides consist mostly of questions for one reason—they are intended to spark conversation rather than fill-in-the-blank answers. In one sense, these discussions are not conventional Bible studies, though they often refer to Bible verses and biblical themes. Instead, consider these sessions as study guides, designed to assist participants in discussing what they feel and think on important spiritual issues.

Each topic is developed around a central point and clear conclusion, but they leave much of the "middle" open to the thoughts of those involved in the discussion. Every person brings perspectives, past experiences, and personal questions to the group. Rather than suppress these individual contributions, each session seeks to draw out the thoughts of each person, comparing the thinking of those in the group with what the Bible communicates in order to point members toward spiritual growth.

Much of the group's success will be determined by its leader(s). Those coordinating the group can also find additional material for each session at the Contenders series website at www.contendersseries.com. At the website, leader(s) will find suggested articles, additional facts, and suggested answers for many of the questions in each session. (Individual participants in your group are welcome to use these resources as well.) In addition, a personal daily study in the AMG Following God™ series called *Defending Your Faith* is available for those who desire a more in-depth study that can be used in combination or separately from these group guides.

In addition, you may want to keep the following list of suggestions in mind as you prepare to participate in your group discussions.[1]

1. The Contenders series does not require that the topics be discussed in an exact order. The guides, in addition to the topics within each guide, can be utilized in any order or even independently of each other, based on the needs of your group or class.

2. It is important to read over the material before each meeting (especially for leaders). The more familiar you are with the topic, the better your ability to discuss the issue during the actual group experience.

3. Actively participate in group discussion. The leader of this group is not expected to share a lecture, but to encourage each person to share in dialogue. This includes both points of agreement and disagreement.

Plan to share your beliefs openly and honestly.

4. Be sensitive to other people in the group. Listen attentively when others share and affirm whenever possible. It is important to show respect for the opinions of others even if they don't agree with your position. However, it is likewise important to affirm the biblical truths of each topic in wrapping up each area of discussion.

5. Be careful not to dominate the conversation. Feel free to share, but be sensitive to the length of time that you share in relation to the input of others in the group.

6. Stay focused on the discussion topic. Discussion can easily digress into side topics that may be equally important, but are unrelated to the session in discussion. As a leader, feel free to say: "That's a good issue to discuss. We should talk about that more sometime, but we need to get back to the topic for this session."

7. Encourage group participants to bring a Bible with them. While we believe there is no "perfect" Bible translation, we believe it is important to be sensitive to the needs of seekers and newer believers in your group by at least including a contemporary translation such as the New International Version or New Living Translation that can help provide quick understanding of Bible passages. Many good study Bibles with helpful notes are also available today to help group members in their growth. In these guides, the New International Version has been used unless otherwise noted.

8. Invest some extra time reading in the Bible, other

recommended resources, or related audio and video content as you work through these sessions. The "Additional Resources" section at the back of each guide provides several such resources to enhance your growth.

The Greatest of These Is Love

Christianity is all about Christ. The very Son of God left the glory of heaven, was born of a woman, lived among ordinary people like you and me, and died a horrific death, before His resurrection and ascension back to heaven. Shortly before His death, He shared with His followers, "Greater love has no man than this, that he lay down his life for his friends" (John 15:13). Jesus provided a perfect example of this love by offering His life for us. As the apostle Paul later wrote, "Now these three remain: faith, hope, and love. But the greatest of these is love" (1 Corinthians 13:13).

As we learn to "contend for the faith," it is of utmost importance that we live with this same overwhelming love to those we encounter. The Christian faith provides more than ample evidence for the hope that we have in Christ. We invite you to explore these life-changing truths with others in a small-group context that leads to even further growth in your spiritual journey. May God bless you as you pursue the truth of Christ and "contend for the faith."

Setting the Stage: How Can We Know God Exists?

An increasing number of books in our time have taken a militant and confident stand that God does not exist. In fact, during the years 2006–2007, bestselling books on atheism have sold nearly one million copies. These included some 500,000 hardcover copies in print of Richard Dawkins' *The God Delusion*, 296,000 copies of Christopher Hitchens's *God Is Not Great: How Religion Poisons Everything*, 185,000 copies of Sam Harris' *Letter to a Christian Nation*, 64,100 copies of Daniel C. Dennett's *Breaking the Spell: Religion as a Natural Phenomenon*, and 60,000 copies of Victor J. Stenger's *God: The Failed Hypothesis: How Science Shows that God Does not Exist*.[2]

But staggering sales statistics are not the only new factor in today's atheism. In *God Is Not Great,* for instance, Hitchens suggests that all religion teaches hatred of unbelievers and feeds the onslaughts found in the worst of extremist groups from the past and present. Others have suggested that religious teaching to children is the equivalent of child abuse.

On the other hand, other skeptics have admitted that to believe in God's existence or to hold to religious values is not necessarily evil. The more common perspective among atheists and other skeptics is that God is either an imagined concept of the masses or that God's existence is unknowable.

Yet such perspectives fail to address the innate universal quest for God overwhelmingly found in the majority of people throughout human history. In reality, there is no question bigger than whether an all-powerful God exists. If God does not exist, then life holds no divine purpose. We are each free to live as we choose. But if an ultimate Creator does exist, then it is appropriate to attempt to discover who He is, what He is like, and if and how He can be known.

The answers to such questions as "Who am I? Why am I here? What is my life's purpose?" can only be found if there is an all-knowing Being who can reveal these mysteries. Without God, these longings are nothing more than a disease of which we must rid ourselves. The existence of God provides a purpose, and possibly even a relationship, for our human existence.

Some scoff at such a quest for truth. Surely such hopes are only wishful thinking, aren't they? How could anyone claim to know for certain that God exists? Even if He does, how could a person know Him personally? Why would a God who is so seemingly unreachable care about the individual aspects of our lives?

To further this struggle, many individuals confuse a view of God, the eternal Father, with their views of their own fathers. When a person experiences a painful childhood or lack of a father figure, that negative image may be projected onto God, creating a God he or she would not want to know in the event He does exist.

Yet for those who begin to investigate the evidence for God's existence with an open mind and a desire for truth, there is much information to consider. The existence of God has occupied the minds of history's greatest thinkers. In addition to whether God exists, there are the follow-up questions of, "What is God like?" and "Does God care for us as individuals?" Perhaps most importantly, we find ourselves inwardly asking, "Can we know God personally? Does He really love me?"

Our hope is that these sessions will stimulate deep dialogue that probes the assumptions of every person in your group. We each have areas for growth and further understanding, regardless of our current spiritual condition. In the end, our goal is that you will have a more accurate and profound perspective of who God is and what He is like and that you will contemplate knowing and experiencing Him. We look forward to the discovery that will take place as you begin your discussions on, "How can we know God exists?"

Is God Really out There?

Getting Started

Wouldn't it be great to know for *sure* that God exists?

One of the greatest and most intense discussions of leading thinkers throughout history has been the debate over whether God is really out there. Today the discussion continues. Even among some of the world's leading scholars, there remains serious skepticism over whether God is simply a human construct or a divine concept.

Why do some people believe with certainty that God does not exist, while others believe with the same level of certainty that He does? To make the issue more personal, what do *you* believe about God's existence? If you believe God does exist, *how* do you know? If you believe He doesn't, how did you make your decision?

We live in a culture where stories about God, Santa, the Tooth Fairy, the Easter Bunny, princesses and princes, Charlie Brown, Winnie the Pooh, and other popular characters are read at bedtime side-by-side. Sometimes the impression is left that God is simply another story character, but not the one and only all-powerful divine being who created the universe. We grew up thinking of God as someone to ask for help, but were then taught to live independently and take care of our own needs. As a result, many leave God behind as a distant memory of childhood.

Yet the concept of a higher power runs deep in our world. Studies have shown that over ninety percent of Americans today say they believe in a divine God or some type of higher power. One Gallup poll has shown that as many as ninety-five percent of all Americans claims to believe in some kind of God, a perspective that has remained rather constant over the past six decades.[3] But is this belief a result of childhood training, personal study, or an unexplained innate feeling? Maybe we *want* to believe there is a God, but we've never really taken a look at the information that shows whether He is real or not.

"The idea of an all-powerful divine being is present everywhere, if not consciously recognized, then unconsciously accepted. Therefore I consider it wiser to recognize the idea of God consciously; otherwise something else becomes god, as a rule something quite inappropriate and stupid." —Carl Jung[4]

Those who struggle the most with the existence of a loving God are often those who have suffered personal injustices that seem to prove there is no one beyond this world who cares for us. "How could a loving God allow my child to die?" or "Why did my mother have to get cancer?" or "Couldn't God have stopped that hurricane from destroying our city?"

SESSION 1

In many cases, God as we have vaguely defined Him does not fit our circumstances. Therefore, some people conclude He doesn't exist at all—at least for them personally.

What do you believe about God's existence? How sure are you about your belief? Is your belief based on intellectual study, faith, or a combination of factors? These are complex questions that are worthy of our thoughts and discussion.

In this session, we invite you to take time to review how you came to believe in or deny God's existence, discover where others are on the journey, and explore new ideas that will further your understanding of who God is. Ultimately, we hope to help address your concerns regarding the question, "Is God really out there?"

Talk about It

1. What were you taught as a child about who God is? What are some of the ways your thoughts about God have changed since then?

2. What have been some of the major influences regarding your current view of God? If you were to list the top three influences on your view of God, who or what would they be?

Here's What I'm Thinking

The Varieties of Views on God

Many people think that the possible answers to the question of God's existence are "Yes," "No," or "Maybe." However, philosophers and theologians have developed a full menu of views regarding God's existence. Below are some of the common ones:

Atheism	God does not exist.
Agnosticism	I don't know if God exists.
Theism	God does exist.
Deism	God exists, created the universe, and has left it alone ever since.
Polytheism	There are multiple gods.
Pantheism	Everything is God.
Absolute Pantheism	Everything is God, and each person believes, "I am God."

3. Which of the above views is the most common among the people you know? Which is the least common view? Why do you think this is the case?

4. How certain do you think your friends are about their views of God? How much thought or study do you think has been given to the issue?

5. How do you think most people decide what they believe about God's existence? Give reasons for your answer.

6. What level of study have you previously pursued to investigate your view of God? Do you feel it is enough? What else do you still desire to learn?

"The greatest question of our time is not communism versus individualism; not Europe versus America; not even the East versus West. It is whether men can live without God."
—Will Durant[5]

What Atheists and Agnostics Say about God

Atheism has always had its vocal supporters. Here are a few quotes from some of them:

> The idea of a personal God is quite alien to me and seems even naive.
>
> —Richard Dawkins, in *The God Delusion*[6]

> Imagine the consequences if any significant component of the U.S. government actually believed that the world was about to end and that its ending would be glorious. The fact that nearly half of the American population apparently believes this, purely on the basis of religious dogma, should be considered a moral and intellectual emergency.
>
> —Sam Harris, in *Letter to a Christian Nation*[7]

> The man who, without prejudice, reads and understands the Old and New Testaments will cease to be an orthodox Christian. The intelligent man who investigates the religion of any country without fear and without prejudice will not and cannot be a believer.
>
> —Robert Ingersoll, considered America's most famous agnostic of the 19th Century[8]

> When I reached intellectual maturity, and began to ask myself whether I was an atheist, a theist, or a pantheist; a materialist or an idealist; a Christian or a freethinker, I found that the more I learned and reflected, the less ready was the answer; until at last I came to the conclusion that I had neither art nor

part with any of these denominations, except the last. . . . So I took thought, and invented what I conceived to be the appropriate title of "agnostic."

> —Thomas H. Huxley, a British skeptic
> who invented the term agnostic
> in the mid-19th Century[9]

My view is that if there is no evidence for it, then forget about it. An agnostic is somebody who doesn't believe in something until there is evidence for it, so I'm an agnostic.

> —Carl Sagan[10]

7. What common themes do you observe in the above quotes? How convincing are these perspectives in your opinion?

8. Why do you think those who don't believe in God are sometimes so vocal in their opposition?

Atheism on eBay

In January 2006, DePaul University graduate student and committed atheist Hemant Mehta listed his services on the eBay auction site. What services? Mehta promised to attend one hour of church for every ten dollars of the final bid.

OfftheMap.org purchased the atheist's services for $504 and sent Mehta on his assignment to attend churches throughout the Chicago area. With an open mind, an outsider's perspective, and a dose of humor, Hemant has been reporting his findings on Off the Map's "Atheist Blog."[11]

9. If an atheist attended your church, what report would he or she give?

10. What approaches are most helpful in talking about God with a person who claims to be an atheist, agnostic, or skeptic?

The Arguments for Atheism

What evidence is needed to prove God *doesn't* exist? The arguments for atheism are largely negative, although some can be cast in positive terms. Four major logical arguments often used by atheists to show that God does not exist include:

1. the fact of evil;
2. the apparent purposelessness of life;
3. random occurrence in the universe; and
4. the First Law of Thermodynamics—that "energy can neither be created or destroyed"—as evidence that the universe is eternal and needs no Creator.

If you think about it, these proposed arguments against the existence of God leave several unanswered questions. The most significant of these questions are:

- *Why is there something rather than nothing?* Atheism does not provide an adequate answer as to why anything exists when it is not necessary for anything at all to exist. Nonexistence of everything in the world is possible, yet the world does exist. Why? If there is no cause for its existence, there is no reason why the world exists. Philosopher John Paul-Sartre said the basic philosophical question is, "Why is there something rather than nothing?"

The 2001 Canadian census data showed that the percentage of "Atheists, Agnostics, Humanists, adherents of no religion, etc." category rose from 12.3% in 1991 to 16.2% in 2001.[12]

- *What is the basis for morality?* Atheists can believe in morality, but they cannot *justify* this belief. Why should anyone be good unless there is a Definer of goodness who holds people accountable? It is one thing to say that hate, racism, genocide, and rape are wrong. But if there is no ultimate standard of morality (as found in God), then why should we

consider these things to be wrong? Who makes up
the rules? A moral prescription implies a Moral
Prescriber.

- *What is the basis for meaning?* Most atheists believe
life is meaningful and worth living. But they can't
tell you why life is meaningful if there is no ultimate
purpose for life, nor destiny after this life. Purpose
implies a Purpose-Maker. But if there is no God,
there is no objective or ultimate meaning. Yet most
atheists propose a purpose and live as if it were true.
It forces the question, "Why is their purpose true?"

- *What is the basis for truth?* Most atheists believe
that atheism is true and theism is false. But to state
that atheism is true implies that there is something
that is really true and something that is really false.
This assumes there is some ultimate standard by
which we can determine what is ultimately true or
false. Most atheists do not believe that atheism is
true only for them. But if atheism is true, what is its
ultimate standard for what is true and false? Truth is
a characteristic of a mind, and objective truth implies
an objective Mind beyond our finite minds—God.

- *What is the basis for reason?* Most atheists pride
themselves on being rational. But why be rational if
the universe is the result of irrational chance? There
is no reason to be reasonable in a random universe.
As a result, the very thing in which atheists most
pride themselves is not possible apart from God.

- *What is the basis for beauty?* Atheists also marvel at
a beautiful sunset and are awestruck by the stars in
the sky. They enjoy the beauty of nature as though
it were meaningful. Yet if atheism is true, it is all
accidental, not purposeful. Atheists enjoy natural
beauty as though it was meant for them, and yet they

believe no Designer exists to mean it for them.[13]

If everything that exists is the result of chance, plus time, plus the impersonal, nothing more, then how can the atheist show we are of more value than a rock, a drop of water, or dirt? Only if there is a personal God who made us is there reason to believe our individual personalities are of value and importance.

11. How many of the four arguments for atheism are based on scientific evidence? How many are based on emotion or observation?

12. Do you think the existence of evil means God cannot exist? Why or why not? What about purpose in life? Do think atheists have overstated their claim that there is evidence that proves God does not exist?

Not All Atheists Stay Atheists

World-renowned scholar Dr. Antony Flew, the world's fore-most philosophical atheist, recently announced his belief in God. His new book, *There Is A God*, highlights how his friendship with C.S. Lewis and numerous debates with Christian scholars influenced his philosophical change.

In fact, some years before Dr. Flew became a convert, I (John) invited him and Christian theologian Dr. Gary Habermas to appear on *The John Ankerberg Show* to debate the evidence for the existence of God, and more specifically, the evidence for the resurrection of Jesus from the dead. (The three-hour debate can be ordered at johnankerberg.org.) After the debate, conversations continued between Drs. Habermas and Flew and myself. Later, we also published a book together on the issue called *Did Jesus Rise from the Dead?*

Habermas and Flew continued to dialogue in the years following this debate. In April 2004, Flew informed Dr. Habermas that he simply "had to go where the evidence leads." As a result of the traditional philosophical and scientific arguments offered by theists, he felt compelled to change his mind from atheism to theism.

13. How open do you think most atheists and agnostics are to changing their view about God's existence? In what ways does the willingness to investigate their position reveal personal bias in their view?

13. A change in view from atheism to theism is a huge transition, but does not necessarily make a person a Christian. What are some of the differences between a person saying he believes in God and a person saying he is a follower of Christ?

15. How certain are you about your particular view of
    God? What would help you feel more certain about
    your perspective?

What Now?

16. Sometimes, atheists claim that those who believe
    in God do so only on faith—without any evidence.
    However, we choose acts of faith every day, including
    our faith that a chair will hold us when we sit down,
    that the sun will rise and set, or that our car will
    start when we turn the key (at least most of the
    time!). What additional examples of everyday faith
    can you think of?

17. Agnostics argue that God's existence cannot be
    proven beyond a shadow of a doubt. Do you need
    one hundred percent proof to believe in God? What
    about other areas of life? For example, how much
    faith do you need in an airplane's safety before you
    will fly in it? What do you think is a reasonable
    amount of faith to believe in God?

Consider This

This session is the start of an investigation into the evidence for God's existence. You are not expected to have all of the right answers. The only expectation is to have an open viewpoint and a desire to learn. In fact, you are probably involved in this study right now due to your curiosity to discover answers regarding some of your own doubts, or at least the doubts of others in your life. Rather than pretending to have the issues all figured out, feel free to express some of your difficult questions and concerns as you continue with this group. The only way to find the answers to your questions is to ask the real questions that still exist in your own mind.

To help identify ways your viewpoints or beliefs are growing during these sessions, throughout this series you will have moments to express where you currently stand on this journey. As you continue to learn, you may find some of your opinions changing from one session to the next. The key idea to remember is that this is a time of growth rather than a test. The more time you invest seeking the truth regarding God's existence, the better your understanding will become on the issues discussed in this guide.

18. Which of the following statements best describes your personal perspective about who God is? (Circle all that apply.)

   A. God does not exist.

   B. I don't know if God exists.

   C. I believe in God or a higher power.

   D. I believe in God but want to know more about the evidence for his existence.

   E. I believe that Jesus is God and have placed my trust in him.

   F. Other thoughts: _____

How Can We Know God Is Real?

Getting Started

How can we know God is real? We simply begin with what is around us.

For instance, we wake up and look outside to see the sun, sky, and clouds. How did they get there? We didn't make them. Something deep inside of us suggests they were made somehow. They couldn't just appear from nothing, could they?

We encounter numerous examples of this thinking every day. When we see a new sports car, we know it was intentionally designed. It didn't just appear one day. The same is true when we study for a test and pass it. The knowledge didn't spontaneously appear (Though you may have tried this option in the past!). We had to study and review the material in order to produce it for the exam.

In addition to the known, physical world, there are also numerous examples of things that are unseen, yet clearly exist. Take the wind, for example. We can feel its effects, but we do not see it. We can turn on a radio and hear a station playing music because of unseen radio waves. Microwaves also function via unseen waves. How do our cell phones know we have a call? Through unseen signals in the air. What about love? Can we see it? Just because we do not physically see these things does not mean they do not exist.

God, as an unseen entity, must fit into this category as well. He exists in a way our five senses do not fully comprehend. For some people, this lack of physical connection proves to them that God does not exist at all. "I can't see God, taste him, touch him, hear him, or smell him. Therefore, He is not there."

However, many people understand that this may be an extreme reaction. Maybe God could exist in a way we could sense through another method, perhaps through intuition or experiencing the supernatural? And even if God did not reveal Himself in these unseen ways, perhaps we could at least observe something about Him through His created universe, sort of like playing detective, moving from known to unknown.

"Logically, since all religions contradict each other, there are only two options open to us. Either they are all false, or there is only one true religion. If there is only one God—there will be only one religion."
—Dr. Robert Morrey[14]

For instance, in an American court of law, the longstanding tradition is that the defendant is innocent until proven guilty. The task for the plaintiff is to prove beyond a reasonable doubt that the defendant has committed the crime he or she is accused of committing. There is no need for the plaintiff to press for one hundred percent proof. The legal case transpires with human elements, not scientific formulas. All that must be established is that the evidence demonstrates that a crime has been committed and that the defendant is the perpetrator.

In this session, we'll take a look at God's existence from this same perspective. We won't claim to make a one hundred percent mathematical deduction to prove God. Instead, we will inductively investigate the evidence for God's existence, examine many of the classic arguments suggested for God's existence, and ask how compelling these arguments are in our desire to know whether God is real.

The decision is ultimately up to you as you take a serious look at the discussion along the way. Is there enough evidence for God's existence to point toward a reasonable belief in God? Begin your discussion and find out!

Talk about It

1. What are some examples of unseen forces or things in our world that we are unable to detect with our human, physical senses?

2. What are some of the reasons you believe (or do not believe) in God's existence?

SESSION 2

Here's What I'm Thinking

The Creation Argument

One of the most powerful lines of reasoning for God's existence has been the argument centered around creation. The
basic idea of this argument is that since there is a universe, it
must have an initial cause beyond itself. It is based on the law
of causality, which says that every limited thing is caused by
something other than itself. There are two different forms of
this argument. The first form says that the universe needed a
cause at its beginning. The second form argues that it needs a
cause *right now* to continue existing.

● *The universe was caused at the beginning*

This argument says that the universe had a beginning.
Therefore, it is finite. It was caused by something beyond the
universe. It can be stated this way:

1. The universe had a beginning.
2. Anything that has a beginning must have been
    caused by something else.
3. Therefore, the universe was caused by something
    else, and this cause was God.

The only way to avoid this argument is to suggest the universe
is eternal; it never had a beginning—it just always existed.
However, this assumption has largely been abandoned as a
result of the scientific evidence for the Big Bang which states
that the universe (all energy, matter, space, and time) had a
beginning. Further, scientists say that a transcendent causal
agent (outside of space and time) brought our universe into
existence. Another name for science's transcendent causal
agent is the personal God of the Bible.

● *The universe needs a cause for its continuing
existence.*

Something has not only caused the world to come into being, but also continues to provide its existence in the present. The world needs both an originating cause and a sustaining cause. Colossians 1:17 tells us, "He [Christ] is before all things, and in him all things hold together."

3. On a scale from one to ten, how compelling is the argument from creation to you? Why?

4. Scientific proof is based on the assumption that a process can be repeated in a lab. This is impossible with the creation of the universe. How does this impact your ability to believe in God?

5. How does the idea that the universe has always existed strike you? Does this seem possible or far-fetched? Ask someone in your group to name the second law of thermodynamics.[15] What is it? How does that law affect your response?

The Design Argument

The design argument argues from design toward an Intelligent Designer. For example, if we walk along the beach and come across the words in the sand, "I love you. Hope to see you soon," we assume an intelligent being wrote that message. It didn't just organize itself by the water swirling around the sand. If we see a beautiful watch on the floor, we immediately realize it was designed and created by an intelligent designer.

This line of thought includes three parts:

1. All designs imply a designer.
2. There is great design (or complexity) in the universe.
3. Therefore, there must be a Great Designer of the universe.

The book of Ecclesiastes notes, "As you do not know the path of the wind, or how the body is formed in a mother's womb, so you cannot understand the work of God, the Maker of all things" (11:5). This verse affirms the same concept—that the complexity of the known universe demands a highly intelligent Designer.

6. Why do you think the concept of Intelligent Design is such a controversial issue in today's fields of science?

7. Could a person logically believe in Intelligent Design and still not believe in God? Why or why not?

8. How convincing is the argument from design for you personally? Why?

The Moral Law Argument

The moral law argument suggests:

1. All people have an innate sense of right and wrong.
2. An innate sense of right and wrong implies an ultimate creator of right and wrong.
3. Therefore, there must be a supreme creator of moral law.

Moral laws are distinct from natural laws. Natural laws describe what is seen; moral laws describe what should be. People may differ regarding particular standards of right and wrong, but there are several points of general agreement. For instance, love, generosity, and loyalty are considered positive values that all people appreciate and respect. On the negative side, acts such as rape, murder, and robbery are generally agreed upon as wrongful actions.

In making such judgments, even though people disagree on specifics, people innately believe in a transcendent moral law which therefore requires a moral lawgiver. When someone cuts us off in traffic and we say, "That's not fair!" who decided that it was not fair? Where did that belief originate?

Paul reveals a biblical perspective on this issue by stating:

> For ever since the world was created, people
> have seen the earth and sky. Through
> everything God made, they can clearly see
> his invisible qualities—his eternal power and
> divine nature. So they have no excuse for not
> knowing God.
>
> Yes, they knew God, but they wouldn't
> worship him as God or even give him thanks.
> And they began to think up foolish ideas of
> what God was like. As a result, their minds
> became dark and confused. Claiming to be
> wise, they instead became utter fools. And
> instead of worshiping the glorious, ever-living
> God, they worshiped idols made to look
> like mere people and birds and animals and
> reptiles. (Romans 1:19–23, NLT)

Through both the physical creation and moral laws, Paul
taught that God has made His existence clear to all people.
Another author has noted:

> It is possible for a person to contend that a
> poem is nothing but black marks on white
> paper. And such an argument might be
> convincing before an audience that could
> not read. You can examine the print under a
> microscope or analyze the paper and ink but
> you will never find something behind this
> sort of analysis that you could call "a poem."
> Those who can read, however, will continue
> to insist that poems exist.
>
> My argument against God was that the
> universe seemed so cruel and unjust. But
> how had I got this idea of just and unjust? A

man does not call a line crooked unless he
has some idea of a straight line. . . . Thus, in
the very act of trying to prove that God did
not exist—in other words, that the whole of
reality was senseless—I found I was forced to
assume that one part of reality—namely my
idea of justice—was full of sense.[16]

9. How convincing is the argument from design for you
    personally? Why?

10. The moral law argument is based on an inward sense
    of right and wrong. Does this inward focus make it a
    weak argument from your perspective? Why or why
    not? How could the moral law argument be seen as
    complimentary to the arguments from creation and
    design?

11. The moral law states that all people have a sense of
    right and wrong. Why do you feel so strongly that
    other people should not steal from you or lie to you?

12. How can people have a sense of right and wrong
    and yet hold to such different standards of right and
    wrong in various areas of life? Do these differences
    regarding *what* is considered right or wrong weaken
    the moral law argument? Why or why not?

The Being Argument

What is the being argument? The being argument (also called
"the argument from being") claims that God must exist by
the very fact that we can actually think of an idea of a perfect
God. Why?

A simple explanation is that we cannot think of things that
could not possibly exist. For example, a person could dream
up green milk, which does not exist. However, the elements
involved, green and milk, do exist. When applied to God, this
argument suggests that we may not know what God is like,
but the very fact that we can conceptualize an ultimate being
called God means there must be an ultimate God of some
kind. For example, God is all-loving. He knows everything.
He is everywhere at once.

This coincides with what Ecclesiastes 3:11 shares: "He
[God] has made everything beautiful in its time. He has also
set eternity in the hearts of men; yet they cannot fathom what
God has done from beginning to end." In other words, we as
humans have a sense of eternity and destiny hardwired within
us. Where did this come from? The being argument says it
comes from God.

14. How convincing is "the argument from being" for
    you personally? Why? Of the four arguments shared

in this session, which one stands out as the most important to you?

15. Why do you think all people long for a sense of purpose or destiny? How does a clear purpose enable us to better live our lives?

16. Why would God say, "The fool says in his heart there is no God" (Psalms 14:1)?

The Most Powerful Evidence

There are three additional ways God could make Himself known very clearly in our world. First, He could change the lives of other people around us. Second, He could change us. Third, He could show up and live among us.

If you consider yourself a follower of Christ, realize that God has already accomplished all three of these things. He has changed the lives of countless people throughout history, probably including at least one person who shared God's love with you.

God has also personally changed *your* life, whether in small or possibly big ways. This experiential change is described in 2 Corinthians 5:17: "This means that anyone who belongs to Christ has become a new person. The old life is gone; a new life has begun!" (NLT). A changed life is often the most powerful way we can show someone that God is real.

"Even if one does not believe in God, there are elements of the idea of God that remain in us." —Jean-Paul Sartre[17]

However, God has taken the evidence one step further. We are also told that He came down and lived among us in the form of His son Jesus Christ: "The Word [Jesus] became flesh and made his dwelling among us" (John 1:14). The original language in this phrase indicates that Jesus literally "pitched His tent" or made His home among us.

16. In another place, Jesus said, "Anyone who has seen me has seen the Father" (John 14:9). What did that mean to any upstanding, orthodox Jew who listened to Him?[18]

17. How can our own changed lives be used as evidence that God is real?

18. In what ways can the life of Christ as recounted in the Bible be used to show that God really exists?

What Now?

19. If you consider yourself a follower of Christ, would your life reveal enough evidence in a court of law that your life is distinctly different from those who do not follow Christ? Why or why not?

20. How does this session's information about the evidence for God's existence increase your confidence in the reality of God?

Consider This

On a scale of one to five, what response best describes your personal beliefs regarding God's existence? (**Hint:** Just because you may not strongly believe all of the evidence for one particular argument does not mean you doubt God's existence.)

21. I believe that God exists because there is no other adequate explanation for the creation of the known universe.

1	2	3	4	5
Don't believe	Believe somewhat	Some of it is true	Mostly true	Completely accurate

22. I believe that God exists because there is no better explanation behind the complexity in our universe:

1	2	3	4	5
Don't believe	Believe somewhat	Some of it is true	Mostly true	Completely accurate

23. I believe that God exists because all people have an innate sense of right and wrong:

1	2	3	4	5
Don't believe	Believe somewhat	Some of it is true	Mostly true	Completely accurate

24. I believe that God exists because of the very fact that we can conceive the idea of an ultimate God:

1	2	3	4	5
Don't believe	Believe somewhat	Some of it is true	Mostly true	Completely accurate

25. I know for certain God exists because he has
    changed my life and the lives of other people:
1	**2**	**3**	**4**	**5**
Don't	Believe	Some of	Mostly	Completely
believe	somewhat	it is true	true	accurate

26. I believe that God exists because He revealed Himself
    through His only Son, Jesus Christ:
1	**2**	**3**	**4**	**5**
Don't	Believe	Some of	Mostly	Completely
believe	somewhat	it is true	true	accurate

What Is God Like?

Getting Started

We live in a culture that often communicates that there are many ways to the same God. However, if we simply read what each religion teaches, we discover that each religion has a distinct view of who God is. These views often conflict with the views of other religious groups. For example, in Christianity, God exists in three entities, including Father, Son, and Holy Spirit, yet all three entities equal one and the same God. (This is referred to as the doctrine of the Trinity.) In Islam, God is one and called Allah. According to Buddhism and Hinduism, there are many gods. So even if we believe in the existence of an ultimate Creator God, we have to define who that God is and what He is like.

Worse, many people who claim to believe in God at a surface level have no interest in getting to know Him. Why? One reason is their perception of who God is. If God is a taskmaster, watching out for our every wrong move to swiftly judge our faults, why would anyone want to know Him?

To be honest, each of us has our own view of who God is. We could sit together in a conversation of ten people and have ten distinct opinions on who God is and how He operates. However, if God is real, then He must have a distinct personality and set of characteristics that belong to Him regardless of what we think. But how do we discover accurate information regarding who God really is? Does He *want* us to know who He really is?

Some resort to mystical, inward experiences. Whether through music, chant, prayer, solitude, or other form of sacred communication, mystic-types desire to know who God is by some type of direct contact with him.

Others are more observational in approach. In other words, some of us discover who we *think* God is by what we observe both in nature and people. If God is anything like His creation, we should be able to better understand who He is by observing what He has made.

This perspective makes logical sense, but sometimes leads to disaster. For instance, a person who claims to follow God, whether Christian or otherwise, may live in a way contrary to who God is. Those who observe the person's actions may make the wrongful assumption that God must be like the actions of that person, even when the actions are contrary to God's nature. If a Christian, for example, cheats on his wife, an outsider could make the observation that a disloyal Christian suggests that God is disloyal, even when this is not the case.

The common term for this type of activity is *hypocrisy*. When a person doesn't live out the faith in God he or she claims to have, it misleads outsiders who are seeking information about who God is and what He is like.

But according to the Bible, knowing God requires a relationship with Him. Developing a relationship with a person— whether with God or anyone else—requires learning more about what he is like.

In this session, we will explore some of what the Bible says regarding who God is. In doing so, we'll find that God is bigger than any book—even the Bible—can contain. Yet in the Bible, God discloses the best and most specific information about Himself. If we read it closely, we can discover amazing insights about who God is and how He desires to work in our lives today.

Talk about It

1. To begin your discussion, have each person write down five characteristics of God's nature. Have each person share his or her five and note which ones are mentioned most frequently. Why do you think these common traits come to mind most often?

2. What do you think are some of the most common misconceptions about God in our culture?

3. How can our views of God help show that not all religions lead to God? What are some of the major differences you know of between the God of the Bible and the gods of other religions?

SESSION 3

Here's What I'm Thinking

What Does the Bible Say about Who God Is?

Theologians who study the Bible talk about what they call "the attributes of God." Dr. Charles Ryrie lists the following categories in his classic book *Basic Theology*:[19]

Eternity	Endlessness	Psalms 10:2
Freedom	Independent of His creation	Isaiah 40:13–14
Holiness	Separate from all that is common or unclean	John 17:11
Immutability	God is unchanging	Malachi 3:6; James 1:17
Infinity	God has no boundaries or limits	1 Kings 8:27
Love	God has no selfishness and cares for creation	1 John 4:8
Omnipotence	God is all-powerful	Genesis 17:1
Omnipresence	God is everywhere at once	Psalms 139:7–11
Omniscience	God is all-knowing	Acts 15:18
Righteous	God exhibits perfect justice	Psalms 11:7

Simplicity	God is a single being, but exists in three persons consisting of Father, Son, and Holy Spirit	John 4:24
Sovereign	God is supreme; above all	Ephesians 1:11
Truth	God is consistent with Himself in all things	John 17:3
Unity	God is one God; not many	Deuteronomy 6:4

Is this a comprehensive list? Probably not. God's attributes include far more than any one list can hold. However, these traits are some of the more common ones listed by experts that are valuable for our investigation into what God is like.

4. Which of the attributes in the above chart are the easiest for you to understand? Which ones do you find most difficult?

5. Some suggest that many religions follow the same God by identifying common traits of God that are consistent in multiple religions. For instance, God is considered all-powerful in Christianity, Judaism, and Islam. Having limitless power is one thing. How it is used is another. Does agreement in only some

SESSION 3

attributes of God mean Christians and Muslims worship the same God? Why or why not?

6. Others argue that the Bible is a human book. Therefore, we cannot trust it to provide accurate information about who God is. Which of the attributes in the chart could be true even for those who do not accept the Bible?

7. After observing the attributes of God from the Bible, does this view of God appeal to you? Why or why not?

8. Theologians often classify God's attributes into two categories; those we can also practice and those which only God can perform. Which of the attributes in the above list should we strive to live out if we claim to be followers of Christ?

Practical Atheism

Even if we believe in God's existence and agree with what the Bible teaches He is like, it does not necessarily change who we are. Some have identified the lifestyle of living as if God does not exist "practical atheism." In other words, we live as if God is not there, watching and listening, and will not someday hold us accountable.

Yet in 1 Samuel 16:7 God says: "The LORD does not look at the things man looks at. Man looks at the outward appearance, but the LORD looks at the heart" (NASB).

God not only made us; He looks at our hearts. He can peer directly into our thoughts and desires.

9. What are some ways or areas in your life in which you tend to live as if God is not watching?

10. What practical steps could you take to help avoid living a life that resembles practical atheism (such as accountability or supportive friends)?

What God's Names Communicate

In the Bible, several names are used in reference to God. Each one describes a particular aspect of who He is. Some of the more common names include:

- *Adonai* (Hebrew word for "Lord" or "master"; Joshua 5:14)

- *Despotes* (Greek word for "master"; Acts 4:24)
- *Elohim* (Hebrew word meaning "strong one"; Genesis 1:1)
- *Kurios* (Greek word for "Lord"; Matthew 5:33)
- *Pater* (Greek word for "Father"; John 4:24)
- *Theos* (Greek word for "God"; Matthew 1:23)
- *Yahweh* (Hebrew word meaning "I am the one who is"; Exodus 3:14)[20]

One author notes: "Unfortunately, to many the names *God* or *Lord* convey little more than designations of a supreme being. It says little to them about God's character, His ways, and what God means to each of us as human beings. But in Scripture, the names of God are like miniature portraits and promises. In Scripture, a person's name identified them and stood for something specific. This is especially true of God. Naming carried special significance. It was a sign of authority and power."[21]

11. Why do you think different parts of the Bible use different names in reference to God? How do these names and their meanings influence or enhance our understanding of what God is like?

12. What do references to God as "Lord" indicate? Why is it significant to understand what God is like in relation to our personal lives?

The Elephant Concept

There is an old Indian tale that is used to help explain the concept of God. It is said that once upon a time a king gathered a few men who were born blind. They were asked to describe an elephant, but each one was presented with only a certain part of it. One person touched only the trunk, another the ears, still another the tail. They quarreled among themselves as they described what they had touched, claiming that all of the others were wrong. The moral presented from the story is that the elephant is a unity of many parts, a unity they could not grasp having only been exposed to a small portion.[22]

This example has also been used to suggest that world religions form a unity, though each religious system observes only one part of the united whole. While this is a message that often resonates with our culture, is the elephant concept compatible when it comes to our view of God?

13. In what ways is this elephant tale incompatible in the area of religion? Why do many people continue to accept this idea that we are all talking about the same God despite this incompatibility?

14. A more accurate word picture is that we each see one perspective of the world and often argue that our perspective is the only correct one. But even if we are incorrect, there is still only one elephant, a true object, despite our flawed thinking about it. How do we sometimes see only a small portion of who God is?

The Triune God

Christian theologians note that the biblical concept of the Trinity reveals God's desire for community. Though God is one in nature, He exists as three in person—Father, Son, and Holy Spirit, each in perfect relationship and unity with one another.

According to the *New Bible Dictionary*:

> So if God is a fellowship within himself he
> can let that fellowship go out to his creatures
> and communicate himself to them according
> to their capacity to receive. This is what
> happened supremely when he came to redeem
> men: he let his fellowship bend down to reach
> outcast man and lift him up. And so because
> God is a Trinity he has something to share: it
> is his own life and communion.[23]

15. In what ways do the relational aspects of the Trinity provide insights into what God is like? How does this encourage us as human beings in our relationships with God?

What Now?

16. Based on the information shared in this session, what are some of the most important discoveries you have made regarding what God is like?

17. Some people say that our view of God determines how we live our lives. In what ways is this true? What changes do you desire to make to expand your view of God?

Consider This

Read the following statements and circle the response that best describes your opinion:

18. The God of the Bible...
    A. is the same as the god(s) of other religions.
    B. is distinctly different from the god(s) of other religions.
    C. shares many similarities with the god(s) of other religions.
    D. I'm not sure what I believe on this issue.
    E. OTHER: _____

19. The attributes of the God of the Bible...
    A. are beyond human comprehension.
    B. are best revealed in the Bible.
    C. are the same in many different religious systems.
    D. I'm not sure what I believe on this issue.
    E. OTHER: _____

20. The names of God...
    A. add very little to my understanding of God.
    B. each emphasize an important aspect of who God is.
    C. I'm not sure what I think about this issue.
    D. OTHER: _____

21. The Trinity...
    A. is a vital Christian concept that highlights the relational aspect of who God is.
    B. is an unimportant concept.
    C. doesn't help me much either way.
    D. I'm not sure what I think about this issue.
    E. OTHER: _____

Are Miracles Possible?

Getting Started

The Bible describes many miracles. From the very first sentence, we are exposed to the tremendous miracle of the creation of the universe. The prophets of the Old Testament make stunningly accurate predictions of future events. Jesus heals people on numerous occasions, and even comes back from death by His own power. The Bible ends with a miraculous scene in which God creates a new heaven and new earth for Christ and his followers to dwell in for eternity.

But just because the Bible says miracles happen, does that mean they are true? Many people have asked this question throughout the centuries. Sometimes we speak of miracles in a very general sense—"It's a miracle I made it to work on time today!" On other occasions, we see amazing accomplishments, such as the 1980 U.S. Olympic ice hockey team's victory, later turned into a film named *Miracle*. When people recover from injuries or sicknesses in unexpected ways, this is also sometimes labeled a miracle.

In some ways, whether miracles are possible or not depend on what a person defines as a miracle. But the miracles of the Bible were different from a sports comeback or an unexpected quick recovery from a sickness. Biblical miracles were always events in which the laws of nature were temporarily altered in dramatic ways.

"One of the unique features of Christianity is that its teachings are built directly upon God's miraculous acts on behalf of his people."[25]

For example, in Exodus, the people of God crossed the Red Sea that was supernaturally parted and became *dry land*. That doesn't just happen, no matter how strongly the wind blows. Noah loaded up a boat with his family and animals, and they became the only survivors in a devastating flood. Joshua stopped the sun for an entire day. Jonah was swallowed by a fish, remained alive for three days in his stomach, and lived to tell about it.

These things don't just happen. They defy the laws of nature. This is what we typically call a miracle.

However, those who reject the occurrence of miracles sometimes ask, "Then why don't similar miracles continue to occur?" When is the last time you've seen someone walk on water? Part a river? Walk out of a fiery furnace without a single burn mark? Did God stop taking miracle orders after the Bible was written, or should we continue to expect others today?

It hasn't helped the situation when a handful of today's religious leaders have claimed miracles of various sorts that have been proven false. It doesn't take very many false miracle stories to turn a curious seeker into a serious skeptic in the area of miracles.

The situation worsens when a person experiences a significant personal loss. *If God could miraculously heal my dad, then why did he have to die in that car accident? Why did I miscarry?* Couldn't God have done a miracle to fix these situations? Why does a loved one have to suffer a prolonged, painful end to life if God can intervene to change the scenario?

This session cannot begin to examine every miracle listed in the Bible. However, we can take the time to determine whether miracles are possible. What we'll find is that miracles cannot be dismissed without a serious investigation into the evidence. Those who refuse to investigate bypass the questions of those sincere seekers who desire to know whether miracles *have* taken place and *can* take place in our world today.

Talk about It

1. Why do you think many people have a difficult time believing that miracles occur? What would it mean if miracles do occur?

2. What types of events do you consider a miracle? For instance, is a person with cancer who suddenly goes into remission an example of a miracle? Or is it only a miracle when the laws of nature have clearly been changed, like when Moses parted the Red Sea?

Dealing with Bias in the Discussion of Miracles

What can be said to the person who believes that miracles *never* happen? Dr. William Lane Craig responded in an interview I (John) taped, stating,

> Since the story of the Gospels is, from start to finish, a story of miracles—the virgin birth, the incarnation, the exorcisms, the healings, the clairvoyant knowledge of the future, prophecy, the resurrection of Jesus—anyone who comes to the text with that presupposition [that miracles never happen] is, of course, going to be forced to discount vast tracts of the text as being unhistorical. But it's important to see that this conclusion is not based on the evidence. It's built into the *presupposition*. If you come to the Gospels with the presupposition of naturalism, then, of course, what you wind up with will be a purely human Jesus. So the issue there isn't one of evidence. The issue there is one of presuppositions. What is the justification for this presupposition of naturalism?[24]

Instead of assuming miracles have never happened, why not investigate the historical evidence *first* to see if there is any reason to believe they do? According to a separate interview I conducted with New Testament scholar Dr. Darrell Bock,

> If you come to the text and you believe miracles can't happen, you kind of have a dilemma on your hands. You read these texts about Jesus multiplying the loaves or you read these texts about Jesus healing the blind, and you have to come up with some

kind of explanation of what goes on. In fact, the healing of the blind is an interesting one because in the Old Testament, blind people didn't get healed. No one did that miracle. And that's not one you can very easily fake.

Every scholar I (John) have interviewed on the issue of miracles has agreed in this area. For instance, Dr. William Lane Craig remarked,

> It would be bad methodology to simply dismiss these [miracles] in advance before even looking at the evidence that they might have actually occurred. Otherwise, we could be ruling out the true hypothesis simply on the basis of a philosophical presupposition [or personal bias, such as, "I have never seen a miracle, therefore miracles have never happened,"] for which we have no justification.

3. In what ways does bias determine how a person views the issues of miracles? How have you seen this in the lives of people you know? In your own life?

4. If we evaluate the historical evidence for a miracle, how much evidence is enough to prove a miracle has taken place?

5. Does personal bias make it impossible to determine the truth of whether miracles occur? Why or why not?

What Is the Purpose of Miracles?

Another important question regarding whether miracles occur is the *purpose* of why they do occur. What is a miracle's purpose? Theologian and philosopher Dr. Norman Geisler suggests that biblical miracles were used to confirm issues of truth. As such, miracles in the Bible largely cluster around one of the three following categories:

- **Prophetic confirmation:** God frequently confirmed messages He gave to prophets in the Bible by performing a miracle. The calling of Moses offers a clear example:

  Moses answered, "What if they do not believe me or listen to me and say, 'The LORD did not appear to you'?"

  Then the LORD said to him, "What is that in your hand?"
  "A staff," he replied.

  The LORD said, "Throw it on the ground."

  Moses threw it on the ground and it became a snake, and he ran from it. Then the LORD said to him, "Reach out your hand and take it by the tail." So Moses reached out and took hold of the snake and it turned back into a staff in his hand. "This," said the

LORD, *"is so that they may believe that the*
LORD, *the God of their fathers—the God*
of Abraham, the God of Isaac and the God
of Jacob—has appeared to you." (Exodus
4:1–5)

- **Messianic Confirmation:** The Bible also notes that
  the miracles of Jesus were to confirm that He was the
  Messiah, God's Son:

  Now there was a man of the Pharisees named
  Nicodemus, a member of the Jewish ruling
  council. He came to Jesus at night and said,
  "Rabbi, we know you are a teacher who has
  come from God. For no one could perform
  the miraculous signs you are doing if God
  were not with him." (John 3:1–2).

Nicodemus was convinced that Jesus was from God because
of the miracles He performed. In another place in the Gospels,
Jesus was asked for an additional confirming sign by the religious leaders (Matthew 12:38). Why? This was expected by
the person who would be the Messiah. Jesus' ultimate miracle
was coming back to life from the dead.

- **Apostolic Confirmation:** Paul, himself an apostle,
  noted:

  "The things that mark an apostle—signs,
  wonders and miracles—were done among
  you with great perseverance" (2 Corinthians
  12:12).

Paul claimed that his work as an apostle had been verified or
confirmed by the many miracles God did through him, something the other apostles were also known for doing in their
ministries (Hebrews 2:3–4).[26]

6. Why do you think it was important for God's prophets, Jesus, and the apostles to be able to perform miracles? How did this help confirm that their work was from God?

7. Some argue that using the Bible to show that miracles occur is unacceptable since they do not believe in the accuracy of the Bible itself. In what ways could this be true? In what ways does this claim reveal the person's bias regarding miracles?

8. In John 10:25, Jesus said that the miracles He had performed spoke for Him. What did His miracles communicate about Him? Why do you think many people were still unconvinced that Jesus was the Messiah during His earthly ministry?

Outside Evidence for Miracles

*   Indicators from Psychiatry and Medicine

Additional support for the existence of miracles has also started to surface in the fields of psychiatry and medicine. In an interview, philosopher and theologian Dr. Gary Habermas revealed,

> I think another factor in favor of the miracles in the New Testament is that there is some very hard data I think that is difficult to explain away. I think of Marcus Borg who reports in one of his books on Jesus that there was a team of psychiatrists recently who could not explain a couple of [demon] possession cases by normal scientific means. I also refer to a double blind experiment with almost 400 heart patients in San Francisco where they were monitored in 26 categories and those who were prayed for were statistically better in 21 out of 26 categories. Because the experiment was performed well, this was published in a secular journal, *The Southern Journal of Medicine*.

> So, if you can see some of these things today, maybe you can't say, "Oh, there's a miracle right there" but it makes you wonder a little bit. I have to say, can we be so quick to condemn the things Jesus did in the first century?

- **Indicators from Science**

Dr. William Lane Craig has noted,

> It's interesting to note that in modern science, for example, in physics, scientists are quite willing to talk about realities [such as the Big Bang] which are quite literally metaphysical in nature—realities which are beyond our space and time dimensions; realities which we cannot directly perceive or know but

which we may infer by certain signposts of transcendence in the universe to something beyond it.

In other words, the scientific community has begun to become more open to the possibility that miracles could occur. For instance, if all matter, energy, space, and time had a beginning, then that original creation was from outside of the known universe. If such a supernatural event could happen once, it is at least theoretically possible from an honest scientific perspective that a similar act, which we would commonly call a miracle, could occur again.

"Despite the difficulty which miracles pose for the modern mind, on historical grounds it is virtually indisputable that Jesus was a healer and exorcist." —Dr. Marcus Borg of the Jesus Seminar, in A New Vision[27]

According to William Lane Craig, "If there is a Creator and Designer of the universe, who has brought it into being, then clearly he could intervene in the course of history and perform miraculous acts. So in the absence of some sort of a proof of atheism, it seems to me that we have to be open to the possibility of miracles."[28]

9. How does the above information from medicine and science help build the case that miracles can and do occur? Does this information prove miracles happen or at least suggest they are possible? In what ways do you personally find this additional information valuable?

10. Why do people who believe in a start to the universe have to at least be open to the possibility of miracles? How could you use this idea in speaking with someone who was skeptical of miracles?

What Now?

11. Have you ever experienced an event in your life that you would call a miracle? What happened?

12. If the Bible is really God's Word, why do you think he hasn't removed the miraculous accounts that appear to some people as contradictions?

13. Why do people who believe in God's existence sometimes not also believe that miracles take place? Do you think that their belief is based on logic, personal experience, or a combination of factors? Do you think it would be possible for God to do a

SESSION 4

miracle for you sometime in your life? Why or why not?

14. Why is Christianity considered a supernatural faith? Could Christianity exist without miracles? Why or why not?

Consider This

Select the choice that best represents your opinion right now regarding the following statements:

15. I believe that miracles...
    A. do not occur.
    B. occurred in the past but do not occur today.
    C. still occur today, but are rare.
    D. happen frequently in our world today.
    E. I'm not sure what I believe about miracles.

16. I believe the miracle accounts in the Bible...
    A. are completely made up.
    B. include a combination of fact and fiction.
    C. are completely true.
    D. I'm not sure where I stand on this issue.

17. Miracles in my life:
    A. I have never personally experienced an event that I would call a miracle.
    B. I may have experienced situations that I would call miraculous, but am not sure.
    C. I have definitely experienced miracles in my life.

Is God Involved in Our Lives Today?

Getting Started

Over 300 million people now live in the United States. The world's population far exceeds six billion. With such a vast number of people living today, does God really care for us individually?

For instance, when we fly in airplanes, we can look down through the windows and see cars and homes that appear the size of specks. Yet each car and home contains one or more people with a complete set of thoughts, feelings, actions, and relationships. As humans, we each have a limited circle of people that we care for and know deeply. Is this how God operates? Does He have a select few that He is close to while other people are more distant? How involved is He?

People who accept the idea that some kind of God exists in the universe do not necessarily agree that God is involved in our daily lives. Certain groups think or prefer God to be a distant creator who simply designed the universe, wound it up like a clock, and let it tick on its own without outside interference.

Of course, views on this issue are often tied to how we have been raised to think about God. For instance, if we are raised to believe God loves us and that we can communicate directly with Him through prayer, we will be more likely to believe God does care about us personally. However, if we are raised to live independently and as if God doesn't really matter, it is easier to wonder if God cares about us at all.

Regardless of our particular conditions in our developing years, it is important to evaluate what we currently believe to see how it matches up with reality. Just because we were raised to think a particular way does not necessarily mean that belief pattern is true.

For example, most of us are told stories about Santa Claus from an early age. Somehow, he is able to fly around the world in one night, visit every home, and deliver exactly the right gifts based on our lists and our behavior over the past year. The story holds up for a while, but at some point our questions become impossible to answer.

Is our attitude about God similar? Are we told one story as a child only to grow up to discover He's really something different?

The Bible mentions God's involvement with various people throughout history, but that was thousands of years ago. Even if it happened then, does it still happen now? Does God really still care about us individually?

In the end, each of us is just a small speck in the universe. Can God really care for us on a personal level? If God does exist, does He really care about us?

This session will explore these questions using the words of Jesus. He takes issue with many other religions when He teaches that God is always there and does care for our daily needs. We'll discover that just as God cares for other parts of creation, such as trees and oceans, He cares much more for the human lives He has created.

Talk about It

1. Have you ever felt that even if God existed, He felt far away and distant? What was happening in your life to make you feel that way?

2. How much do you think God personally cares about you and your life? What influences have led you to this view?

Here's What I'm Thinking

If God Cares So Much about Birds...

Jesus once provided an insightful commentary that reveals God's care for the people He has created:

> Look at the birds of the air; they do not sow or reap or store away in barns, and yet your heavenly Father feeds them. *Are you not much more valuable than they?* Who of you by worrying can add a single hour to his life?
>
> And why do you worry about clothes? See how the lilies of the field grow. They do not labor or spin. Yet I tell you that not even

SESSION 5

Solomon in all his splendor was dressed like
one of these. If that is how God clothes the
grass of the field, which is here today and
tomorrow is thrown into the fire, *will he not
much more clothe you*, O you of little faith?
So do not worry, saying, "What shall we
eat?" or "What shall we drink?" or "What
shall we wear?" For the pagans run after
all these things, and *your heavenly Father
knows that you need them.* But seek first his
kingdom and his righteousness, and all these
things will be given to you as well. (Matthew
7:26–33, italics added)

God cares for birds to the point that He provides them with
their daily food. He also cares that individual lilies grow and
blossom with beauty. Jesus continues by stating that, yes, God
cares a lot about birds and flowers, but he is also our heavenly Father and cares **much more** about each of our personal
lives.

3. Why do you think many people believe that God
    does not care about them personally?

4. How did Jesus challenge His listeners to live as a
    result of God's intimate concern for our individual
    lives? In what ways could this apply to a concern you
    are facing in your life today?

God's Lost Causes

In Luke 15, Jesus shares three different stories on the single theme of God's response to lost people. Most people today don't like to be told they are lost. If someone visited a church and heard that the church was "praying for the lost," they might wonder who had run away from home. For a large portion of our population, the word "lost" brings to mind a TV show rather than a biblical concept.

However, the tradition of talking about lost people is connected with these three episodes shared by Jesus. Here is a summary of each of them:

- *A Lost Sheep*: Jesus lived in a culture in which shepherding was a common job. In this account, Jesus shares that a shepherd has 100 sheep and realizes one is missing. Instead of saying, "Oh, well, I still have 99," he sets off on a search and rescue mission for his missing sheep. When he finds it, he asks his friends to celebrate with him the fact that his lost sheep is now home.

   In this story, Jesus specifically shares, "I tell you that in the same way there will be more rejoicing in heaven over one sinner who repents than over ninety-nine righteous persons who do not need to repent" (v. 7).

- *A Lost Coin*: In Luke 15:8–10, Jesus next tells of a woman who has ten coins and loses one. She sweeps and cleans her house until she finds it. Then she invites her friends over for a party to celebrate the fact that she has found it.

   Why was finding a coin such a big deal to this woman? The coin mentioned was worth a full day's wages. Take the amount a person in America makes in one day of work.

At a $40,000 annual salary, for example,
that equals approximately $153 per workday.
Would you be concerned if you misplaced
that much money? Wouldn't you be excited to
find it again?

● *A Lost Son*: In Luke 15:11–31, Jesus raises the stakes
by speaking of a lost son. In this account, a father
has two grown sons. One asks for his inheritance
early, which he wastes in a distant town on his
own self-focused desires. Broke, the son takes a job
feeding pigs. At this low point, he decides to return
home and humbly ask his father if he can work as a
servant for him.

When he returns, the father's response is
startling: ". . . his father saw him and was
filled with compassion for him; he ran to
his son, threw his arms around him and
kissed him" (v. 20). He orders an immediate
celebration in honor of his son's return.

After the faithful son who did not leave
home becomes upset, the father reminds him
that, ". . . we had to celebrate and be glad,
because this brother of yours was dead and
is alive again; he was lost and is found" (v.
32). The emphasis in this story is the father's
unconditional love toward his son, regardless
of the son's actions.

5.   What common themes do you find in these three
stories? What one major concept is expressed that
connects the three accounts?

6. What common reactions do all three stories include when the missing item is found?

7. What do these three accounts teach about God's love for individual people? For your life?

Every Last Detail

Matthew 10:30 tells us that God knows so much about us that He has numbered every hair on our heads. This verse expresses God's ultimate concern for every detail of our lives. There is nothing in our lives that God deems unimportant. The early church father Augustine taught that God loves each of us as if there were only one of us.

One author puts it this way:

> How wide is God's love? Wide enough for the whole world. Are you included in the world? Then you are included in God's love. God's love is just for you.
>
> It's nice to be included. You aren't always. Universities exclude you if you aren't smart enough. Businesses exclude you if you aren't qualified enough, and, sadly, some churches exclude you if you aren't good enough.

SESSION 5

But though they may exclude you, Christ
includes you. When asked to describe the
width of His love, He stretched one hand to
the right and the other to the left and had
them nailed in that position so you would
know He died loving you.[29]

8. Have you ever considered that God loves you so
    much that He cares about every aspect of your life?
    Why or why not?

9. What do you think of the phrase, "God loves each
    one of us as if there were only one of us"? How does
    that make you feel?

What Now?

10. What is something you have lost that was very
    valuable? How did it make you feel? How did you
    respond? How were your feelings similar to how God
    feels toward people?

11. How difficult is it for you to personally accept that God loves you and cares about you personally? Why do you think this is the case?

12. In what ways does the information shared in this session change your perspective about how God feels about you?

Consider This

13. My childhood view of God's love toward me was. . . . (Check all that apply.):
    ___ that He did not care about me at all.
    ___ that He intimately cared about my life.
    ___ that He did not even exist, much less care about me.
    ___ that His concern for me was based on the right and wrong things I did. He cared, but it was conditional.

14. My current view of God's love toward me is. . . . (Check all that apply.):
    ___ that He does not care about me at all.
    ___ that He intimately cares about my life.
    ___ that He does not exist, much less care about me.

SESSION 5

___ that His concern for me is based on the right and wrong things I do. He cares, but His love is conditional.

15. My desire to tell others about God's love:
   ___ I want to tell everyone about God's love.
   ___ I would like to tell others about God's love, but am scared to do it.
   ___ I want to tell others about God's love, but don't know how.
   ___ I am not very interested or motivated to tell others about God's love.

SESSION 6

How Can We Know God Personally?

Getting Started

What's the difference between *having* a favorite celebrity and *knowing* your favorite celebrity? Everything!

For a favorite celebrity, you may know his or her name, hometown, date of birth, and other trivial facts. You may be able to name the person's favorite food or even the names of every film the person has acted in. Regardless of your level of knowledge about the person, however, you still cannot say you know the person.

Many people regard God with this same celebrity mentality. Sure, we can know a lot *about* who God is. We can study what others have said about Him throughout history or His influence on our world, but know Him? That's different.

But what if we could really know God personally? Just as it is possible to meet a favorite celebrity and appreciate the person even more, a personal encounter with God would further deepen and enhance our view of Him.

In fact, the Bible suggests much more. It tells us that God desires a *personal relationship* with each of us (Romans 5:10–11). But if this is correct, then how do we begin a relationship with God? Do we need to complete a series of steps or perform a certain number of good deeds to start? Should we attend church more, give money to the poor, or go out and sell all of our possessions to serve God among the world's most needy people?

"If [people are] going to say Jesus is not going to be important in [their lives], . . . then they're going to have to say that for other reasons besides historical. . . . the evidence is there, the sources are there, the picture is clear and coherent, and in my academic opinion, the picture is quite compelling."
—*Dr. Craig Evans*

These activities can all be good, but we'll discover in this session that God's desire for a relationship with us is not based on our performance, but on a way he has already designed—a way that includes His only Son, Jesus.

We've discussed various perspectives on whether God exists. We've evaluated the philosophical debates for why an ultimate designer must stand behind our creation. We've highlighted some of the attributes that define who the God of the Bible is. We've mentioned the occurrence of miracles. We've even shared how God cares about our lives at a very intimate, individual level.

Now, we shift one final time to explore what the Bible shares as the way we can know God personally. Why is this important? First, it is essential because our culture communicates that there are multiple ways to know God. Which viewpoint is right? Would a loving God give us an intelligent mind to use and then give thousands of ways to know Him that contradict one another? Wouldn't it be more loving and make more sense if He just gave us one way and marked it clearly?

Second, it is vital to know God personally because it impacts how we live our lives now. For instance, if you know you have a personal connection with the creator of the universe, then your confidence during times of struggle will be much higher. Your sense of purpose and destiny will increase as you realize your part in the unfolding drama of God's plan. Your relationships will take on new meaning as you live each interaction with the perspective that God is there and cares about each nuance of your daily life.

Third, a personal relationship with God is essential because it determines our eternity. Reincarnation or annihilation (the idea that we simply cease to exist upon death) viewpoints offer little comfort. The thought that God exists but that we may not reach heaven to be with Him creates an equal or greater discomfort.

However, those who know God personally live with confidence that this life is not all there is. When we live with the knowledge that there is a greater reality in our future, this life holds greater importance. This divine, eternal perspective changes life for eternity and changes our lives in a positive way for today.

Talk about It

1. Name a celebrity whom you have always wanted to meet. How would you act if you had the opportunity to meet him or her in person?

SESSION 6

2. Name someone you know who lives as if he or she
    has a very close relationship with God. How is this
    person's view of God different from other people you
    know?

3. What do you think keeps people from having close,
    personal relationships with God? Why do you think
    more people do not know God on a personal level?

Here's What I'm Thinking

With God, There Is No Neutral

Have you ever thought, "I don't hate God. I just don't feel
really passionate about Him." Another way to express this
kind of thinking is the concept of a neutral attitude toward
God.

However, the Bible shares that there is no such thing as
living with a neutral perspective toward God. James, the first
leader of the Jerusalem followers of Christ, wrote: "Don't you
know that friendship with the world is hatred toward God?
Anyone who chooses to be a friend of the world becomes an
enemy of God" (James 4:4).

We are each either an enemy of God or a friend of God.
What is the difference between the two? James tells us how to
become God's friend: "Submit yourselves, then, to God. Resist

the devil, and he will flee from you. Come near to God and he will come near to you" (James 4:7–8).

"Therefore, the historian, whether that historian be a secularist, a Muslim, a Christian, whatever—the historian has to ask, 'How do we explain the fact this movement spread like wildfire with Jesus as the Messiah, even though Jesus had been crucified?' The answer has to be, 'It can only be because he was raised from the dead.' "—Dr. N. T. Wright

---

4. On a scale from one to ten, how passionate would you say you are about a friendship with God? Do you feel you have already started a friendship with God in the past, or are you uncertain about your relationship with Him?

5. How can a person submit to God or come near to him? How does the aspect of submission make this relationship different from the relationships we have with other friends?

SESSION 6

If Life Is a Highway...

One of the more popular ways to share how a person can begin a relationship with God is called the Romans Road. Why? The apostle Paul in his letter to Roman followers of Christ shares these key steps in the process of beginning a friendship with God through His Son Jesus:[30]

- **Who is perfect?** "There is no one righteous, not even one" (Romans 3:10).
- **Who has sinned?** "For all have sinned and fall short of the glory of God" (3:23). When Paul uses the word "all," does that include you and me? Whether we like it or not, the answer is, "yes."
- **Where did sin come from?** ". . . sin entered the world through one man [Adam], and death through sin, and in this way death came to all men, because all sinned" (5:12).
- **How can our sin be removed?** "The gift of God is eternal life in Christ Jesus our Lord" (6:23).
- **Who has made it possible for our sin to be removed?** "God demonstrates his own love for us in this: While we were still sinners, Christ died for us" (5:8).
- **How can we know God?** "If you confess with your mouth, 'Jesus is Lord,' and believe in your heart that God raised him from the dead, you will be saved. For it is with your heart that you believe and are justified, and it is with your mouth that you confess and are saved" (10:9–10).
- **How can we know we have started a relationship with God?** "Everyone who calls on the name of the Lord will be saved" (10:13).

6. Which of these verses from Romans is the easiest for you to understand and accept? Which is the most difficult?

7. Why do you think it is important to understand our *need* for a relationship with God in addition to how to know God personally? Which of the verses above do you think is most difficult for many people to accept?

8. Do you think that all of these verses from Romans must be fully understood for a person to begin a relationship with God? Why or why not? If you were to summarize how to begin a relationship with God in one sentence, what would you say?

The Jesus Factor[31]

The primary reason Jesus said He came into our world was to rescue us from divine judgment and provide a way for us to enjoy a close, personal relationship with Him. He promised us we could have our wrongs fully and freely forgiven. Our guilt removed, our joy restored.

SESSION 6

To enjoy these benefits, we are to simply ask for forgiveness from our wrongs (an act of humility) and trust solely in Jesus to save us. How can we know this? From the earliest times, biblical writers have urged:

> Seek the Lord while you can find him. Call on him now while he is near. Let the wicked change their ways and banish the very thought of doing wrong. Let them turn to the Lord that he may have mercy on them. Yes, turn to our God, for he will forgive generously (Isaiah 55:6–7, NLT).

"The claim of the resurrection of Jesus alone makes him unique among the religious figures of the world. The fact that we have good evidence for it makes it more than unique. It makes it astonishing."[32]
—Dr. William Lane Craig

Jesus personally promises each person who will come to Him, "I tell you the truth, those who listen to my message and believe in God who sent me have eternal life. They will never be condemned for their sins, but they have already passed from death into life" (John 5:24, NLT). In a prayer to His Father the night before His crucifixion, Jesus explained it this way: "This is the way to have eternal life—to know you, the only true God, and Jesus Christ, the one you sent to earth" (John 17:3, NLT).

The Compassion of Jesus		
#	Situation	Verses
1	*When he saw the crowds, he had compassion on them...*	Matthew 9:36
2	*When Jesus landed and saw a large crowd, he had compassion on them and healed their sick.*	Matthew 14:14
3	*"I have compassion for these people. . . ."*	Matthew 15:32
4	*Jesus had compassion on them and touched their eyes.*	Matthew 20:34
5	*Filled with compassion, Jesus reached out his hand and touched the man.*	Mark 1:41
6	*... he had compassion on them, because they were like sheep without a shepherd.*	Mark 6:34
7	*"I have compassion for these people. . . ."*	Mark 8:2

The best part about this relationship is that it's not based on the quality of our performance. Jesus certainly wants us to do what is right, but following Him is based on His gift of grace. Our part is to take the step of faith to open this life-changing gift, and then He helps us do what is right.

The apostle Paul described this mystery. He wrote to early Christ-followers that, "God saved you by his grace when you believed. And you can't take credit for this; it is a gift from God. Salvation is not a reward for the good things we have done, so none of us can boast about it" (Ephesians 2:8–9, NLT).

Do you know for certain that you have a personal relationship with God through Jesus Christ? If not, would you be willing to take a moment to begin a relationship with Him right now?

There is no magical prayer to begin a relationship with God. However, for those who desire to begin or affirm a relationship with God, here is a sample prayer that could be used to help begin the process:

> *God, I ask Your son Jesus to enter my life as*
> *my leader and rescuer from my sins. I know*
> *I've messed up. Please forgive me. I believe*
> *Jesus died on the cross, paid for my sins,*
> *and came back to life from the dead. Right*
> *now, I place my faith in Him for eternal life.*
> *I choose to follow Jesus from this moment*
> *forward. Please show me how to live for You.*

9. Why do you think Jesus is an essential part of beginning a relationship with God? How does the fact that Jesus is the only way to God show that other spiritual paths are either incomplete or inaccurate?

10. Do you feel like it is arrogant to suggest there is only one way to have a relationship with God? Why or why not? How can Christianity be exclusive in its requirements and also be loving?

11. What do you believe is your next step to begin or grow in your relationship with God?

12. If someone asked you how you know that Christ is in your life, how you know for sure God will take you to heaven when you die, what would you say? (See Romans 10:13 and 1 John 5:13 again for these answers.)

What Now?

13. On a scale from one to ten, how close do you feel your relationship is with God right now? How could you go about making your relationship with Him closer?

14. What life situations do you think cause people to think more deeply about God? How could this information help you talk with other people about beginning a personal relationship with Him?

SESSION 6

15. When are some times you feel the closest to God? Why do you think this is the case?

Consider This

Answer the following belief statements based on your discussion in this session:

16. I believe that God desires to know me personally:
___ True
___ False
___ Not sure

17. I believe that the only way to have a relationship with God is through His Son, Jesus Christ:
___ True
___ False
___ Not sure

18. I believe that my relationship with God is not based on my efforts or performance but on what Jesus has done on my behalf:
___ True
___ False
___ Not sure

19. I believe it is essential that I develop greater intimacy with God through prayer, Bible reading, and other spiritual practices on a daily basis:
___ True
___ False
___ Not sure

20. Having completed this series, I would like to do the following: (Mark all that apply.)
___ Become a believer in Christ.
___ Recommit my life to Christ.
___ Begin a regular time of Bible reading and study.
___ Continue with another title in the Contenders series of Bible studies.
___ Lead this study or a similar study with some of my friends, coworkers, classmates, or family.

End your final session in a brief time of silent prayer regarding your next step in your spiritual journey. Afterwards, decide as a group what to do next in your desire to continue your spiritual growth.

> *"The true, living faith, which the Holy Spirit instills into the heart, simply cannot be idle."*
> —Martin Luther[33]

Also, don't forget to look at the "Additional Resources" section for audio, videos, internet materials, and books on this issue that can be used personally or as additional group learning tools. In addition, we have provided two appendices for your reference. The first is for those who would like to begin a relationship with God. The second is an outline of Bible verses to help you in praying for other people who have yet to experience the joy of a personal relationship with Christ.

SESSION 6

Finally, please have a representative from your group take a moment to send an email to us via the Contenders series website (www.contendersseries.com) to share highlights from your group with others. We would appreciate any stories of life-change that can be used to encourage others in their spiritual journey. God bless you as you continue growing in your spiritual journey!

APPENDIX A:

How to Begin a Personal Relationship with God

If you would like to begin a personal relationship with God that promises joy, forgiveness, and eternal life, you can do so right now by doing the following:

1. Believe that God exists and that He sent His Son Jesus Christ in human form to Earth (John 3:16; Romans 10:9).
2. Accept God's free gift of new life through the death and resurrection of God's only son, Jesus Christ (Ephesians 2:8–9).
3. Commit to following God's plan for your life (1 Peter 1:21–23; Ephesians 2:1–7).
4. Determine to make Jesus Christ the ultimate leader and final authority of your life (Matthew 7:21–27; 1 John 4:15).

There is no magic formula or special prayer to begin your relationship with God. However, the following prayer is one that can be used to accept God's free gift of salvation through Jesus Christ by faith:

> "Dear Lord Jesus, I admit that I have
> sinned. I know I cannot save myself. Thank
> You for dying on the cross and taking my
> place. I believe that Your death was for me
> and receive Your sacrifice on my behalf. I
> transfer all of my trust from myself and turn
> all of my desires over to You. I open the door
> of my life to You and by faith receive You as
> my Savior and Lord, making You the ultimate
> Leader of my life. Thank You for forgiving
> my sins and giving me eternal life. Amen."

If you have made this decision, congratulations! You have just made the greatest commitment of your life. As a new follower of Jesus, you will have many questions, and this group is a great place to begin. Let your group leaders know about your decision and ask what resources they have available to assist you in your new spiritual adventure.

Other ways you can grow in your new relationship with God include:

- spending regular time in prayer and Bible reading.
- finding a Bible-teaching church where you can grow with other followers of Christ.
- seeking opportunities to tell others about Jesus through acts of service and everyday conversations.

For more information on growing in your relationship with God, please see www.contendersseries.com or www.johnankerberg.org. You can also receive additional materials by contacting the authors at:

The Ankerberg Theological Research Institute
P.O. Box 8977
Chattanooga, TN 37414
Phone: (423) 892-7722

APPENDIX B:

Praying for Those Who Do Not Believe

The Scriptures provide several ways for us to pray for those who do not know Jesus. However, it's often a daunting task to choose where to begin in praying for others. The following outline of verses is designed to assist in offering biblical prayers for those who do not believe.

1. Pray for God to draw the person to Himself.

   No one can come to me unless the Father who sent me draws him. (John 6:44)

2. Pray that the person would desire God.

   But in their distress they turned to the LORD, the God of Israel, and sought him, and he was found by them. (2 Chronicles 15:4)

   God did this so that men would seek him and perhaps reach out for him and find him, though he is not far from each one of us. (Acts 17:27)

3. Pray for an understanding and acceptance of God's Word.

    Consequently, faith comes from hearing the message, and the message is heard through the word of Christ. (Romans 10:17)

    And we also thank God continually because, when you received the word of God, which you heard from us, you accepted it not as the word of men, but as it actually is, the word of God, which is at work in you who believe. (1 Thessalonians 2:13)

4. Pray that Satan would not blind them.

    When anyone hears the message about the kingdom and does not understand it, the evil one comes and snatches away what was sown in his heart. (Matthew 13:19)

    The god of this age has blinded the minds of unbelievers, so that they cannot see the light of the gospel of the glory of Christ, who is the image of God. (2 Corinthians 4:4)

5. Pray that the Holy Spirit would convict of sin.

    When he comes, he will convict the world of guilt in regard to sin and righteousness and judgment. (Matthew 16:8)

6. Pray for someone to share Christ with them.

    Ask the Lord of the harvest, therefore, to send out workers into his harvest field. (Matthew 9:38)

7. Pray that God provides His grace and repentance. (Repentance is a change of mind that leads to changed behavior.)

Repent, then, and turn to God, so that your sins may be wiped out, that times of refreshing may come from the Lord. (Acts 3:19)

For it is by grace you have been saved, through faith—and this not from yourselves, it is the gift of God—not by works, so that no one can boast. (Ephesians 2:8–9)

8. Pray that they believe and entrust themselves in Jesus as Savior.

Yet to all who received him, to those who believed in his name, he gave the right to become children of God. (John 1:12)

I tell you the truth, whoever hears my word and believes him who sent me has eternal life and will not be condemned; he has crossed over from death to life. (John 5:24)

9. Pray that they confess Jesus as Lord.

That if you confess with your mouth, "Jesus is Lord," and believe in your heart that God raised him from the dead, you will be saved. For it is with your heart that you believe and are justified, and it is with your mouth that you confess and are saved. (Romans 10:9–10)

10. Pray that they continue to grow spiritually and learn how to surrender all to follow Jesus.

Then Jesus said to his disciples, "If anyone would come after me, he must deny himself and take up his cross and follow me." (Matthew 16:24)

"But whatever was to my profit I now consider loss for the sake of Christ. What is more, I consider

everything a loss compared to the surpassing greatness of knowing Christ Jesus my Lord, for whose sake I have lost all things. I consider them rubbish, that I may gain Christ. (Philippians 3:7–8)

So then, just as you received Christ Jesus as Lord, continue to live in him, rooted and built up in him, strengthened in the faith as you were taught, and overflowing with thankfulness. (Colossians 2:6–7)

Additional Resources

Interested in learning more? For those seriously pursuing more on the life of Christ and Christianity, several additional quality tools exist. We have listed below several other resources available from The Ankerberg Theological Research Institute along with a list of helpful websites on the subject.

Ankerberg Theological Research Institute Resources

All of the following Ankerberg resources can be ordered online at www.johnankerberg.org or by phone at (423) 892-7722.

Books

All of the following books are authored or coauthored by Dr. John Ankerberg or Dillon Burroughs:

Ready with An Answer for the Tough Questions About God (Eugene, OR: Harvest House, 1997).

The Case for Jesus the Messiah: Incredible Prophecies that Prove God Exists (Chattanooga, TN: Ankerberg Theological Research Institute, 1989).

Defending Your Faith (Chattanooga, TN: AMG Publishers, 2007).

Fast Facts on Defending Your Faith (Eugene, OR: Harvest House, 2002).

The Facts on Why You Can Believe the Bible (Eugene, OR: Harvest House, 2004).

What's the Big Deal About Jesus? (Eugene, OR: Harvest House, 2007).

Video and Audio Programs & Transcripts

The following topics are available in VHS & DVD format. Most programs offer downloadable transcripts as well.

Dealing with Doubts

The Problem of Evil: Why Does God Allow Evil and Suffering in the World?

What Happens One Minute after You Die?

Why Do Bad Things Happen to Good People?

Online Articles

Over 2,500 online articles on Christianity and comparative religions are hosted on The Ankerberg Theological Research Institute website. For an A to Z directory, see http://www.johnankerberg.org/Articles/archives-ap.htm.

About the Authors

Dr. John Ankerberg is host of the award-winning apologetics TV and radio program *The John Ankerberg Show*, which is broadcast in more than 185 countries. Founder and president of the Ankerberg Theological Research Institute, John has authored more than sixty books, including the bestselling *Facts On* apologetics series, with over 2 million copies in print, and *Defending Your Faith* (AMG Publishers). His training includes three earned degrees: a Master of Arts in church history and the philosophy of Christian thought, a Master of Divinity from Trinity Evangelical Divinity School, and a Doctor of Ministry from Luther Rice Seminary. For more information, see www.johnankerberg.org.

Dillon Burroughs is a research associate for the Ankerberg Theological Research Institute. Author or coauthor of numerous books, including *Defending Your Faith* (AMG Publishers), *What's the Big Deal About Jesus?*, and *Comparing Christianity with World Religions*, Dillon is a graduate of Dallas Theological Seminary and lives in Tennessee with his wife, Deborah, and two children.

Endnotes

1   These guidelines adapted from Judson Poling, *How Reliable Is the Bible?*, rev. ed., (Grand Rapids, MI: Zondervan, 2003), pp. 14–15.

2   Peter Berkowitz, "The New New Athiesm," *The Wall Street Journal*, July 16, 2007. Accessed at http://www.opinionjournal.com/editorial/feature.html?id=110010341.

3   George H. Gallup, Jr., "Gallup Index of Leading Religious Indicators," *Gallup*, February 12, 2002. Accessed at http://www.gallup.com/poll/5317/Gallup-Index-Leading-Religious-Indicators.aspx.

4   Carl Jung (H. G. and C. F. Baynes, translators), *Two Essays in Analytical Psychology* (New York: Dodd Mead, 1928), p. 73, cited in Rollo May, *The Art of Counseling* (New York: Abingdon, 1957), p. 217.

5   Cited in Ravi Zacharias, *The Real Face of Atheism* (Grand Rapids, MI: Baker Books, 2004), p. 19.

6   Richard Dawkins, *The God Delusion* (New York: Houghton Mifflin, 2006). Accessed at http://www.richarddawkins.net/mainPage.php?bodyPage=godDelusion.php.

7   Sam Harris, *Letter to a Christian Nation* (New York: Knopf, 2006), p. 1. Available online at http://www.samharris.org/site/book_letter_to_christian_nation/.

8   R.G. Ingersoll, *Why I Am an Agnostic*, cited at http://www.religioustolerance.org/agnostic.htm.

9   Thomas H. Huxley, *Christianity and Agnosticism: A Controversy* (New York: D. Appleton and Company, 1889). Accessed at http://www.infidels.org/library/historical/.

10   Cited in Mark Water, *AMG's Encyclopedia of World Religions,*

Cults, and the Occult (Chattanooga, TN: AMG Publishers, 2006), p. 483.

11　From http://blog.christianitytoday.com/outofur/archives/2006/04/the_ebay_atheis.html.

12　From http://www.religioustolerance.org/agnostic.htm.

13　Adapted in part from Norman Geisler, "Tenets of Atheism, Part Two," Ankerberg Theological Research Institute, 2003. Accessed at http://www.johnankerberg.org/Articles/theological-dictionary/TD0603W1.htm.

14　Robert A. Morey, *Introduction to Defending the Faith* (Southbridge, MA: Crowne Publications, 1989), p. 38.

15　Hint for the scientifically challenged: the second law of thermodynamics states that energy spontaneously flows only from being concentrated in one place to becoming diffused and spread out. For more, see http://www.secondlaw.com/two.html.

16　Bruce L. Shelley, *Christian Theology in Plain Language* (Nashville, TN: Word, 1985), p. 95.

17　Cited in Simone de Beauvoir, "A Conversation About Death and God," *Harper's* magazine, February 1984, p. 39.

18　Hint: This meant that Jesus claimed to be equal with God. This is why Jesus ended up being put to death. He was accused of claiming to be the Messiah, a king.

19　Charles Ryrie, *Basic Theology* (Colorado Springs, CO: Victor Books, 1986), pp. 36-44.

20　Adapted from Charles Ryrie, *The Ryrie Study Bible: Expanded Edition* (Chicago, IL: Moody, 1995), p. 5.

21　J. Hampton Keathley, III, "The Names of God," *Biblical Studies Foundation*. Accessed at http://www.bible.org/page.php?page_id=220.

22　This full story can be found at http://www.comparativereligion.com/.

23　*The New Bible Dictionary*, Logos Research Systems, Electronic Media.

24　Ken Boa and Larry Moody, *I'm Glad You Asked* (Colorado Springs, CO: Victor Books, 1982, 1994), p. 49.

25　All of the quotes from this section can be found in the DVD and related transcript "Jesus: the Search Continues," *The John Ankerberg Show*, 2002.

26　These categories are from Norman Geisler, *Baker Encyclopedia of Christian Apologetics* (Grand Rapids, MI: Baker, 1999), pp. 454–455.

27　Marcus J. Borg, *Jesus, A New Vision: Spirit, Culture, and The Life of Discipleship* (San Francisco, CA: Harper San Francisco, 1991), p. 61.

28   All of the quotes from this section can be found in the DVD and related transcript "Jesus: the Search Continues," *The John Ankerberg Show*, 2002.

29   Max Lucado, *He Chose the Nails: What God Did to Win Your Heart* (Nashville, TN: Word, 2000). Accessed at http://www.gnpcb.org/product/663575725350.

30   Adapted from romansroad.org.

31   This section is adapted from the conclusion of our book *What's the Big Deal About Jesus?* (Eugene, OR: Harvest House, 2007).

32   From "A Response to ABC's *The Search for Jesus*," on *The John Ankerberg Show*, 2001.

33   From http://www.bible.org/illus.php?topic_id=526.